S.S. 448.

FOR OFFICIAL

METHOD OF INSTRUCTION

IN THE

$$\frac{40}{\overline{\text{W.O.}}}{3650}$$ # LEWIS GUN.

Issued by the General Staff, May, 1917.

The Naval & Military Press Ltd

Printed and bound by CPI Antony Rowe, Eastbourne

INDEX.

During hours of instruction, except at the actual firing point on the range, live ammunition must never be brought near the Lewis Gun. Thus, in time allotted to filling magazines, the guns must be removed from the squads.

Two kinds of dummy cartridges are issued by Ordnance for instructional purposes :—

    (1) Wooden dummies to show the movement of the ammunition inside the gun, action of feed mechanism, stoppages, &c.

    (2) Metal dummies, for use as tools in stripping.

The authority for the issue of these dummies is G.R.O. 2065. Dated 7.1.1917.

(B 12744) Wt. w. 3039—9797 30M 6/17 H & S P 17/51

SECTION 1.

General Description.

Name :—
 Lewis Gun. ·303 in. ; gas operated and air cooled.
Weight :—

 Gun, 26 lbs. Magazine $\begin{cases} \text{Empty } 1\frac{1}{2} \text{ lbs.} \\ \text{Full } \quad 4\frac{1}{3} \text{ lbs.} \end{cases}$

 Bipod mounting, 2 lbs.

The Gun is worked by two forces :—
 (a) The force of the gas.
 (b) The return spring.

Explain briefly :—
 (a) How gun is loaded and fed
 (b) How gun is fired.
 (c) How gas operates piston and moving portions.
 (d) How return spring operates piston and bolt
 (e) How gun is cooled.

 NOTE.—*Do not talk too much about things that cannot be seen, wait for these until gun is stripped.*

The Gun is divided into two portions :—
 (1) The stationary portions.
 (2) The moving portions.

The Stationary Portions consist of :—
 (a) The Barrel Group.
 (b) The Body Group.

 (a) The Barrel Group consists of :—
  (i) *The Barrel.*—Calibre ·303 in. ; number of grooves, 4 ; twist of rifling, right-handed.

   NOTE.—*For purpose of demonstration the spare barrel should be shown.*

   It is threaded at the muzzle to take the *barrel mouth-piece,* which has a left-handed thread to prevent it from working loose, or being detached from the barrel during the firing.

   A gas vent is bored in it 4 inches from the muzzle to allow the gas to pass into the gas cylinder. A square thread is cut at the rear end for attachment to the *body*

A

A stud in front of the square thread fits in a slot in the radiator, ensuring the gas vent being in position to receive the gas chamber.

At the rear end of the barrel is a projection which coincides with the cut away portion of the bolt face when the bolt is closed ; the rim of a cartridge bears against it in order to give room for the extractor to clip over the rim.

The upper part of the entrance to the chamber is grooved to direct the nose of the bullet downwards.

(ii) The *radiator* is of aluminium, is split longitudinally, and sprung on to the barrel.

It assists in dissipating the heat of the barrel. A *recess* for the gas chamber is provided at the forward end, and a *flat* which corresponds with one on the *radiator casing* is made at the rear end to assist in alignment.

(iii) The *radiator casing* consists of front and rear portions which are connected by a *clamp ring*. The rear portion has a hole cut in it to allow the entrance of the gas regulator.

A *flat* is provided at the rear end to correspond with the flat on the radiator, and the rear face is drilled to admit the barrel and gas cylinder, and also the body locking pin.

The front portion is tapered and extends beyond the barrel mouthpiece.

On both portions are slots to take the stud on the clamp ring. The *clamp ring* is turned up at both ends to form a foresight protector. and the inner portion on right side forms the foresight *block*, and is dovetailed to receive the foresight. It is held in position by the *clamp ring screw*.

(iv) The *Mark I gas chamber* screws into the *barrel band* which fits round the barrel, and fits into a recess in the barrel, which is cut round the *gas vent*.

The rear face of the *gas chamber* is threaded to receive the *gas cylinder* and tapped for the *gas regulator*, and has *wings* which the spanner grips when screwing up.

(v) The *gas regulator* has a large and a small hole marked L and S, either of which can be placed opposite the hole in the rear face of the gas chamber.

It is operated and held in position by means of the *gas regulator key,* for which a recess is cut in the gas regulator.

The key is held in position by a stud on the rear end, which enters a recess in the rear radiating casing. A loop is provided at the rear end of the key, which enables the point of a bullet to be used to spring the key out of the recess.

(vi) The *gas cylinder* is shaped at the rear end to admit the rack on the piston rod. Its forward end screws on to the gas chamber.

NOTE.—*Great care should be taken to guard the threads from injury, and to prevent the flattened portion from being damaged by the rack in stripping.*

When guns are fitted with the Mark II gas chamber and gas cylinder, substitute the following for paragraphs (iv) *and* (vi) *above:—*

The *Mark II gas chamber* embodies a ring which fits round the barrel and takes the place of the barrel band in the Mark I pattern. Its rear end is threaded to take the gas cylinder. It is threaded internally to take the screwed plug. The latter has a left-hand thread, is arranged to take the barrel mouthpiece spanner and has eight holes drilled through the cylindrical portion. It is threaded internally to take the gas regulator. On its upper surface is a nipple which passes up through the ring and seats in the vent hole in the barrel. The plug is kept in position by a keeper screw and the holes in it and the recesses for the barrel mouthpiece spanner are so arranged that when the keeper screw is in one of the recesses one of the holes is opposite the gas cylinder.

(*b*) The Body Group consists of :—

(i) The *body,* which is threaded to screw on to the barrel, is drilled to take the *body locking pin* and a groove is cut, through which the pin is operated when stripping.

Bottom.—Underneath the body is a pin, on to which the *pinion casing* hooks, and openings are cut to allow the *pinion, plunger,* and *sear* to enter.

Grooves are also made to take the pistol grip, and the lower projection of the butt cap.

Sides.—On either side of the gun is an opening in which the shank of the cocking handle can travel. Over each opening is a sliding plate with two recesses, and thumbpiece, as safety catch and dust protector. On the right side is the ejector opening.

Top.—The body carries on top the *magazine post*, which is hollowed and counter-sunk to actuate the magazine catch when placed in position with a key on the exterior, to prevent the centre block of the magazine from rotating.

The top of the body is slotted throughout the greater part of its length, the front part of the slot taking the shape of a cartridge, while the rear portion fits the boss on the feed arm actuating stud.

Near the front end of the cartridge-shaped slot, on its left, is a small-groove which coincides with a depression in front portion of the feed arm. Near the rear end of the cartridge-shaped slot are two projections which keep the cartridge in position until the bullet enters the chamber. At the rear end, on the right side, is a groove into which fits the rim of the cartridge.

The *ejector seating* lies on the left side of the slot, and is closed by a spring cover, and a hole is drilled in the body, into which the stud on the ejector fits, and on which it pivots.

A groove is cut at the rear end of the body, into which the stud on the tail end of the feed arm moves.

Projections are provided to lock the body cover.

Interior.—Inside the body are drilled the *Bolt-way* and the *Piston-way.*

The bolt-way has four grooves in the form of a cross which admit the lugs on the bolt and the feed arm actuating stud.

Recesses are provided at the forward end of the bolt-way, in which the locking-lugs on the rear end of the bolt lie when the bolt is closed. Near the rear end of the bolt-way are recesses in which the interrupted flanges of the butt cap engages.

On the left of the bolt-way slots are cut to allow the ends of the ejector to project alternately into the bolt-way.

The *piston-way* is flat-bottomed to take the *rack.*

(ii) The *body cover* fits on top of the body.

The projecting *Tongue* at the front end has underneath it a seating for the cartridge guide spring. Underneath are the *axis studs* for the *stop pawls.*

Projections to engage under the projections on the body are provided at the sides. Fixed to the top by a screw is the *tangent sight bed.*

The *tangent sight leaf* is hinged to it, and held in position by the *tangent sight spring*.

The *tangent sight slide* is of the aperture pattern, and is actuated by the elevating screw, which is operated by a *milled head*, with a *nib* and *spring*.

The *cartridge guide spring* (or *cartridge guide*) is held in position by an undercut recess, and has a stud which fits in a hole in the tongue. The left leaf is turned over ; in the case of the cartridge guide the right leaf is hinged and operated by a flat spring.

The *stop pawls* pivot on studs, the pawl on the left fitting underneath that on the right. Its head is enlarged to bring it on a level with the underside of the cover.

The *stop pawl spring* lies behind the pawls, and a stud on its back fits in the rib behind it. Part of the left of the spring is turned over to embrace the stop pawl.

(iii) The *pinion casing* is shaped to contain the *pinion* and *spring*. At the front end is the *hook*, which connects it to the body, and at the rear end is the *pinion pawl ;* a rib on one arm of the pawl engages in the pinion and is kept in action by a spring bearing against the back of the arm. The other arm of the pawl projects from the casing, and is lifted by the pistol grip as the latter is slid into position, thus disengaging the rib from the pinion.

The casing is drilled to take the *tension screw*.

(iv) The *pistol grip* consists of a frame which is channelled to contain the *plunger, trigger, sear* and *butt catch*.

It extends to form the *trigger guard* and *pistol grip. Guide grooves* to connect it with the body are cut on the sides of the former. At the forward end is a *recess* for the *pinion pawl*. The *plunger* is a cover for the *trigger spring*, and is slotted to take the front end of the trigger.

The *sear* and *trigger* are both pivoted on *axis pins ;* the *jaw* on the rear end of the trigger controls the sear.

At the rear end is the *butt catch*, with a spiral spring and fixing pin.

(v) The *butt* has on the front face the *butt cap*. Projections are provided for attaching it to the body, also a recess into which the tooth on the butt catch fits.

The Moving Portions consist of :—

(i) The *piston rod*, which is in two parts, and is joined by a loosely-fitting thread, secured by a pin, to compensate for any slight want of alignment between cylinder and body.

The head is cupped and ringed ; the rings tend to make a gas-tight joint.

Under the rear portion of the piston is a *rack ;* behind the rack is a *bent,* which engages with the nose of the sear.

On top is the *striker post,* which is drilled for the *striker,* which is secured by a fixing pin.

A slot for the shank of the *cocking handle* is cut in the rear end.

(ii) The *bolt* has on the face a rim to support the base of the cartridge.

Gaps for the *extractor seatings* are cut in the surface of the bolt.

The extractors are flat springs with a hook on the head to engage the rim of the cartridge. They are fitted with a stud and shoulders, which spring into a recess and a groove on the bolt.

A *slot* is cut in the rim for the head of the ejector.

A *cammed slot* is cut into the bolt in which the striker post travels.

There are four lugs at the rear end to take the shock of discharge, and the rear face is tapped to take the feed arm actuating stud.

The *ejector* is housed in a seating on the left side of the bolt-way. It is pivotted on a stud which fits in a hole cut in the body to receive it. Slots cut in the bolt-way allow the head and tail alternately to project into the bolt-way, the ejector being operated by the bolt as it travels to and fro. The front end is the head and the rear the tail. The rear end is bent in order to allow the left lug of the feed arm actuating stud to strike it as the bolt comes to the rear. It is retained in its seating by a spring cover.

(iii) The *feed arm actuating stud* screws into the rear of the bolt, has *lugs,* which work in the guideways and prevent it from turning, and a *boss* which travels in the long slot in the bolt-way and actuates the feed arm.

(iv) The *feed arm* has an axis hole, which passes over the magazine post, and a recess to clear the key on the post when stripping. A hinged *latch* secures the feed arm to the magazine post by engaging in a cut on the front face of it.

An opening is cut to allow the cartridges to pass from the magazine to the body ; a small depression on its left acts as a bullet stop and keeps the cartridge in position during the movement of the feed arm to the left.

A tongue slightly further in rear prevents the cartridge from jumping up after leaving the cartridge guide spring

Behind this are the *axis, stop and spring retaining studs* for the *feed arm pawl* The *pawl* has a slot in which the spring lies, and underneath is a recess for the stop stud and a stud for the *loop* on the spring.

The *tail* of the feed arm is curved and grooved underneath to receive the boss on the feed arm actuating stud.

At the end of the tail is a *stud* which engages with the top lug of the bolt when the latter reaches its limit of movement to the rear, thus holding the feed arm in position until the boss on the feed arm actuating stud again enters the groove in the tail of the feed arm.

(v) The pinion is bored to admit the tension screw, and has an *internal recess* to correspond with a projection on the spring casing, to lock the two parts.

The *hub* is threaded for the tension screw, and is slotted to take one end of the *return spring*, which is coiled inside the spring casing and attached to it by two studs.

The Magazine.

The *magazine*, which holds 47 rounds, is a circular *pan* with *rectangular indentations* on the rim, inside which are riveted plates to hold the bases of the cartridges. A *ring* carrying 25 *separating pegs* is riveted over a hole which is cut out of the centre of the pan. The pegs and indentations hold the cartridges in position, and force them round when the pan is rotated.

Twenty-five *recesses* for the *nib* on the *magazine catch* are provided inside the ring and pan. A *steel disc* covers the central hole and has a channel cut in it for the magazine catch, which has a hook with sloping head and a projection to engage below the cone on the magazine post.

A spring (*magazine catch spring*) lies in the channel and keeps the nib pressed into one of the recesses in the ring and pan.

A *centre block* with a spiral channel in which the bullet ends of the cartridges lie, is riveted to the centre disc, and keeps the magazine catch in position in the channel.

In the centre is the hole for the magazine post and a *key way* is cut to fit the key on the magazine post. The magazine catch locks the centre block to the pan, and prevents it from rotating when not in position.

To fill by hand :—

　1. Place the magazine bottom upwards on a flat surface.
　2. Insert the loading handle and rotate the centre block or pan, placing the cartridges horizontally in succession between the separating pegs in such a way that the lip of the bullet groove engages them and leads them to place.
　3. Care should be taken not to leave an empty space.

NOTE.—When no loading handle is available, the nose of a bullet, or a charger, may be used as a substitute ; it is a help to place a cartridge vertically in one of the holes of the centre block of the magazine.

SECTION 2.

Stripping.

Special dummy cartridges with steel bullets are issued for use in stripping. Live rounds must never be used for instructional purposes. Many accidents have been caused by this practice.

With the exception of the gas chamber and the barrel mouth-piece for which a spanner has to be used, and the clamp ring, which is taken off with the gas regulator key, the whole of the gun can be stripped by means of the nose of a bullet.

To strip the gun :—

　1. With cocking handle in the forward position, lift the butt catch and remove the *butt-stock* by turning it one-eighth turn to the left.
　2. Press the trigger, and withdraw the *pistol grip* to the rear.
　3. Pull back the *cocking handle* to its fullest extent, and withdraw it.
　4. Remove *bolt* and *piston rod.*

5. With the feed arm over to the right, pull back the *body cover*, and lift it off.

6. Unhook the *pinion casing*.

7. Open the latch, turn the key-way until opposite the key on the magazine post, and lift off the *feed arm*, taking care not to strain it in doing so.

8. Take out the body locking pin, and unscrew the *body* from the barrel.

Care must now be taken to prevent damage to the projections on barrel.

9. Lift *key* out of hole in radiator, and unscrew the *gas regulator*.

10. Unscrew the *clamp ring* and remove the *front radiator casing*, sliding the *rear* part of the *casing* off to the rear.

11. Insert the piston to form a wrench, and unscrew the *gas cylinder*. Care should be taken to insert the piston rod sufficiently far to prevent damage to the rear end of the cylinder.

12. With the spanner unscrew the *barrel mouthpiece* to the right.

The following parts should be stripped as seldom as possible.

13. With the spanner unscrew the *gas chamber* (or screwed plug).

14. Heat the radiator with hot water, drift out the barrel to the rear with a piece of wood, and remove the *band* or *gas chamber*.

Re-assemble in the reverse order.

Note :—

(i) See that the feed arm is over to the right before replacing the body cover, and to the left when replacing the bolt.

(ii) See that feed arm actuating stud is screwed up.

(iii) See that cocking handle is right home and forward before replacing pistol grip.

(iv) See that barrel band is right way on before replacing barrel. A letter " F " indicates the front of the band.

Stripping Various Components.

1. To remove an *extractor*, raise the hook until the stud is clear of the recess in the bolt, and push the extractor out, care being taken not to strain it by lifting it more than is necessary.

2. To remove the *stop pawls*, force the stud on the pawls spring out of its seating and lift the *pawls* off their studs. Note that

the studs and pawls are marked 1 and 2, so as to ensure their being reassembled in the right order.

3. To remove the *cartridge guide spring*, press the stud down and slide the spring out.

4. Raise the rear end of the ejector cover and slide it to the rear to remove the *ejector*.

5. To remove *return spring*, press up the arm of the pinion pawl to release the spring. Unscrew the tension screw.* Allow the pinion to drop out of its casing. With the point of a bullet press on the hub and push the spring casing out of the pinion.

The following should only be carried out when necessary.

6. To remove the *sear*, press out axis pin, and to remove *trigger, plunger or spring*, press out trigger axis pin.

7. To remove *pinion pawl*, push out the axis pin.

8. The *foresight* can be driven out of its bed with a punch through the holes in the foresight protector.

9. To remove the *tangent sight bed* and *tangent sight*, unscrew the fixing screw.

Note :—

(1) After the first few times, stripping should be practised in a sitting or lying position.

(2) When replacing damaged parts, the gun should be stripped as little as possible.

(3) It may be necessary to move the cocking handle slightly when raising the pinion casing into position before the rack will engage with the pinion.

SECTION 3.
Mechanism.

To demonstrate the working of the mechanism, dummy rounds with wooden bullets should be used. To prevent accidents, live ammunition must never be brought near the gun during instruction.

Sequence of Instruction :—
1. Show how to load.
2. Show how to fire.

* If the spring is broken, in order to remove the tension screw it may be necessary to release the pinion pawl and unwind the return spring, at the same time tapping the tail of the tension screw.

3 Action of the gas on the moving portions.

4. Action of the return spring.

5. Single shots and continuous fire.

6. How to unload.

1. Show how to put on the magazine and load.

NOTE.—Show each action as it takes place. Dummies should always be used. The magazine may be removed after the first cartridge has dropped to show the action more clearly.

2. Show that :—

(a) On pressing the trigger, the gun fires and continues to fire until the pressure is released.

(b) On releasing the trigger the gun stops in a fully cocked position, with a live round under the cartridge guide spring.

3. Show that :—

When the powder gases expand through the gas vent into the gas chamber, and pass through the hole in the gas regulator :—

(a) The *piston* is forced back, and the rack on its under-side, rotating the pinion, winds up the return spring and the bent passes over the nose of the sear.

(b) The *striker post* bearing against the cammed slot in the bolt (after the first $1\frac{1}{2}$ inches of travel) rotates the bolt and frees the locking lugs from the recesses in the body, and the rear part of it bears against the cammed slot, forcing the bolt back, till the piston and bolt are back to their full extent.

(c) The *bolt*, by means of the extractors, withdraws an empty case from the chamber, and in its backward travel pushes the tail of the ejector out of the bolt-way, and the head, swinging into the boltway, ejects the empty case.

(d) The *boss on the feed arm actuating stud* carries the feed arm over to the left, and the feed arm pawl, which is bearing against a projection on the magazine, carries the pan round with it.

(e) *A cartridge* is forced down the slope of the centre block. When the bullet end is clear of the lip, it is forced through the cartridge opening in the feed arm on to the top of the body, the tongue on the body cover ensuring this action.

It is carried to the left by the indentations and separating pegs of the magazine, and forced under the cartridge guide spring (or cartridge guide), aided by the right side of the cartridge opening in the feed arm.

(*f*) The *spring retaining stud* of the feed arm pawl, moving to the left, releases the right pawl, allowing the latter to engage in front of the projections on the magazine and preventing it rotating too far ; the left pawl is pressed back by one of the projections on the magazine as it moves to the left, and then comes forward again to prevent any rotation in the opposite direction.

4. Show that :—

(*a*) *Pressing the trigger* disengages the sear from the bent, and the unwinding of the return spring rotates the pinion, forcing the piston rod forward by means of the rack.

(*b*) The *striker post,* unable to rotate the bolt owing to the lugs being in the guide-grooves, carries the bolt forward.

(*c*) The *feed arm actuating stud* is carried forward with the bolt, and the boss carries the feed arm over to the right ; the feed arm pawl passes over a projection on the magazine and engages behind it ; the spring retaining stud presses the right pawl out of the path of the magazine, the left pawl prevents the magazine from slipping back.

(*d*) The *top extractor* during the forward movement of the bolt meets the cartridge and pushes it into the chamber, the cartridge stop and the small depression stop on the feed arm controlling it during the movement. The front of the bolt pushes the head of the ejector out of the bolt-way and the tail swings in.

The extractors spring over the rim of the cartridge as it goes home into the chamber, and the bolt which is now fully forward is able to turn, the lugs being clear of the grooves.

(*e*) The *striker post* now rotates the bolt and turns the locking lugs into the recesses in the bolt-way ; the striker passing through the face of the bolt hits the cap and explodes the charge.

5. Show that :—

(*a*) If the trigger is instantaneously released after pressing it, single, or at times two, shots will be fired according to the rapidity with which the sear rises and engages with the bent.

(*b*) If pressure is maintained the gun will fire until the magazine is empty.

NOTE.—The action of the feed can be more clearly shown as follows :—

Hold the loading handle vertically in the hand and place over it the spare feed arm. This will represent the magazine post of the gun with its feed arm. Then place on the handle a magazine, in which is a dummy cartridge, and show action.

SECTION 4.

Points Before, During and After Firing.

Points before firing :—

(i) Remove oil from the bore.

(ii) Oil all frictional parts behind the body locking pin.

(iii) Weigh return spring (13 to 14 lbs.) with cocking handle in the forward position at the moment when the cocking handle *begins* to move.

(iv) Test the feed mechanism.

(v) Examine magazines and ammunition while filling.

(vi) Examine spare parts.

(vii) See that the barrel mouthpiece is tightly screwed up.

To *increase* the tension of the return spring (after withdrawing the pistol grip sufficiently to allow the pinion pawl to engage in the pinion), press up the pinion casing with the left hand, in order to keep the pinion engaged with the rack, and draw back the cocking handle. Allow the pinion casing to drop so that the pinion is not engaged with the rack, and push the cocking handle forward.

To *decrease* the tension of the return spring, allow the pinion casing to drop so as to disengage the pinion from the rack, draw back the cocking handle, press the pinion casing up to engage the pinion with the rack, and disengage the pinion pawl from the pinion to allow the piston rod to fly forward.

Reassemble and weigh as before.

Points during firing :—

(i) Replace empty magazines in cases.

(ii) Oil bolt and striker post, and also magazine post.

(iii) Weigh return spring.

(iv) Turn gas regulator slightly to prevent seizing of the threads in the gas chamber.

(v) Replace partially-used magazines.

(vi) Send empty magazines back for refilling.

(vii) See that clamp ring is screwed tight.

Points after firing :—

(ı) Unload and press trigger, to ease the return spring.

(ii) Oil the bore.

On return to billets :—

(i) Strip gun and clean thoroughly.

(ii) Carry out any necessary repairs.

(iii) Wash, dry, and oil dirty magazines.

(iv) Examine barrel for metallic fouling and remove as in Sec. 5.

(v) Lower the tension of the return spring to zero.

SECTION 5.

Instructions for Cleaning.

When ball ammunition has been fired, daily cleaning of the barrel is necessary for at least 10 days afterwards. Subsequent cleaning must depend on the discretion of the officer in charge of the gun ; but in situations where the barrel is exposed to a moist atmosphere it must be carried out daily.

The gas chamber, cylinder, regulator and piston rod must be cleaned with the same frequency as the barrel. In order to avoid loosening of the joint between the gas chamber and the barrel by constant stripping, it must not be removed, but will be cleaned while in position on the barrel.

After cleaning, all parts must be left lightly coated with oil.

To clean the barrel.—Pull the cocking handle back till the sear engages. Place a piece of flannelette about 4 inches by 1½ inches in eye of the cleaning rod, *taking care to surround the metal of the cleaning rod with the flannelette*, which must be well oiled. Insert the rod into the muzzle and pass it up and down the bore till all fouling has been removed. Replace the oily flannelette with dry pieces, and finally pass freshly oiled pieces through, leaving the barrel well oiled. If the flannelette is tight and is pushed through the breech it is necessary to reverse it before pulling it back, otherwise it will jamb.

If the chamber has not been properly cleaned by the above process, remove the butt, body cover, pistol grip, piston rod and bolt. Place a larger piece of flannelette in the front eye of the cleaning rod, insert the rod from the breech end and clean the chamber first with oiled and then with dry flannelette.

To use the double pull-through.—If rust or metallic fouling is present in the barrel remove the parts of the gun described in the preceding paragraph. Thoroughly oil the gauze on the pull-through and drop the weight through the bore from the breech. Care should be taken to pull the pull-through through the bore in line with its axis. Continue the motion until the rust or fouling is loosened. The barrel can now be cleaned with the cleaning rod and flannelette as already described. When the gauze fits too loosely to clean the grooves of the rifling its diameter can be increased by inserting under each side narrow strips of flannelette or paper. When the gauze is worn out it should be replaced by one of the spare pieces which are issued with each double pull-through.

To clean the gas cylinder.—Joint up the cylinder cleaning rod and screw on the wire brush. Insert the rod into the gas cylinder and work it backwards and forwards a few times. Then remove the wire brush, replace it with the mop and clean the cylinder. When there is not time to remove the cylinder for cleaning, the foregoing operations can be carried out by removing the bolt and piston rod and inserting the cylinder cleaning rod through the piston rod hole.

To clean the mechanism.—A mixture of equal parts of Russian petroleum and paraffin should be used. If any parts are clogged with dried oil, spirits of turpentine should be used to remove it. After cleaning each part it should be thoroughly dried and slightly oiled with Russian petroleum. Very little oil should be used for this purpose, as it is apt to catch the dust and clog. A little oil should be applied to the magazine catch, and round the exterior of the centre disc.

The exterior of the gun and the exterior and interior of the magazine should be rubbed over with a slightly oiled rag. Any excess of oil in the interior of the magazine is likely to be carried into the chamber.

Protection during gas attack.—The gun must be kept carefully cleaned and well oiled with mineral oil. The effects of corrosion of ammunition are even more serious than the direct effects of gas upon the gun. Magazines should be kept in some form of box, the joints of which can be made gas tight by inserting strips of flannelette.

Occasional short bursts of fire will lessen the chance of guns jamming from the action of gas during a gas attack.

After a gas attack the gun must be cleaned and re-oiled at once;

and at the first available opportunity it should be stripped and all working parts cleaned in boiling water containing a little soda.

SECTION 6.

Examination of Gun.

It is most important that any signs of wear, friction, or play should be at once reported to armourers for adjustment and repair.

Examine :—

Barrel. Condition of bore, rifling and lead, for metallic fouling or erosion. Projections on rear face and thread on muzzle for damage.

Pinion and Casing. Teeth for breakage, pawl and spring for dirt, thick oil, or weakness.

Return Spring for breakage.

Ejector for roughness.

Feed Arm. Latch for weakness, axis hole for play on magazine post, thin portion of arm for bending or strain, stud and groove for wear ; top of feed arm for friction against ribs on body cover. Pawl for wear, and spring for weakness.

Body Cover pawls and spring for damage, and cartridge guide spring for correct assembling.

Piston rod. Joint for excessive play, rack and striker post for damage or wear ; piston head for erosion or carbon deposit.

Bolt. Cammed slot for wear or roughness, studs on extractors and face of bolt for corrosion or rust. Lug on left of feed arm actuating stud for wear or roughness.

Trigger Guard, for lateral play in grooves, sear for wear and plunger for thick oil and dirt.

Gas Regulator for erosion and carbon deposit.

Gas Cylinder for erosion and carbon deposit.

Gas Chamber for erosion and carbon deposit.

Clamp Ring. Screw for wear and ring for tightness on radiator casing.

Tangent Sight Leaf. Elevating screw and slide for damage and spring for weakness.

Body for play at each end, and wear.

Pinion Hinge and see pin is straight.

Butt-cap for marking by piston during recoil and for play.

Magazines. Rims for damage and pan for distortion, by rotating on loading handle.

SECTION 7.

Stoppages.

Position of Cocking Handle.	Immediate Action.	Secondary Action.	If	Cause.
I. In forward position.	Rotate magazine, pull back cocking handle and carry on.	—	—	Misfire due to defective round.
		If the gun still will not fire, remove the magazine, pull back the cocking handle and examine the ejected round.	Ejected round is untouched.	Broken striker.
			Ejected round is marked by striker.	Bad ammunition.
			Empty case is ejected.	No gas.
			No round ejected.	Broken feed pawl or spring or damaged magazine.
II. Over Thumbpiece	Pull back cocking handle, using lanyard if necessary and carry on.	—	—	Hard extraction. Lack of oil or gas. Dirt. Carbon in gas vent, regulator, cylinder or piston.
		Remove magazine—oil gun—turn gas regulator and examine moving parts for brightness.		Defective part in gun. Return spring the wrong weight.
III. Behind the Thumbpiece on Safety Catch.	Pull back cocking handle and carry on.	Pull back cocking handle, raise safety catch and remove magazine. Examine cartridge slot, ejection opening and for broken cartridge guide spring.	One cartridge is half under cartridge guide spring, pull it back and carry on.	
			It occurs again.	Weak cartridge guide spring.
			One cartridge is in cartridge slot and one in ejection opening.	Broken ejector
			One cartridge in chamber and one in ejection opening.	Broken extractor.

SECTION 8.

Additional Notes on Stoppages.

1. *Return spring.*—A very weak or broken return spring may give a stoppage in any position. It is easily recognised by the lack of weight on the cocking handle when performing Immediate Action. When the spring is weak, the gun may stop in No. 1 position ; when it is broken, the gun will probably stop in No. 3 position.

2. *A method of removing a round, which has passed under the tongue when there is an empty case in the chamber, if the clearing plug is not available.*

(a) Draw back the cocking handle and raise the safety catch.

(b) Take a live round in the right hand, with the point of its bullet draw back and depress the base of the round under the tongue.

(c) Seize the bullet of the latter round in the left hand, draw it forward, and place the round held in the right hand, bullet downwards, behind its base.

(d) Lower the safety catch, hold the cocking handle in the right hand, press the trigger with the left hand, and allow the cocking handle to move slightly forward in order to bring the feed arm over to the right.

(e) It will now be possible to pull forward to the right front the round which was caught under the tongue.

3. *Friction, fouling, etc.*—In very bad cases the gun may stop in No. 1 position, owing to friction in the gas cylinder or other working parts of the gun, also owing to the gas regulator or gas chamber being fouled.

Prevention of recurrence.—Clean the breech, cylinder and piston head, also remove gas regulator and fire one shot to clean out gas vent.

4. *Gas regulator key missing.*—This may give either No. 1 or No. 2 position, according to the amount the gas regulator has turned. As a remedy, a piece of wood may be inserted and tied to the radiator casing.

5. *Hard extraction.*—

(a) If, in addition to hard extraction, there is friction in the working parts, or the gas regulator and gas chamber are fouled, the cocking handle may remain in No. 1 position. The gun will then have to be stripped and cleaned.

(b) If it stops in No. 2 position with an empty case in the chamber, the extractor having jumped or the rim being torn, the usual remedy will fail and a No. 3 stoppage will result.

(c) It is possible that, owing to hard extraction, an empty case may be left in the chamber or bolt-way and the bolt may pass behind the base of the next round, causing the gun to stop in No. 3 position.

Prevention of recurrence : Clean the chamber.

6. *Magazines, damaged or broken.—*

(a) If the magazine rim is bent, or the projections are worn, the feed arm pawl will not rotate the magazine.

(b) If the magazine is bent the stop pawl will not engage in front of a projection, a No. 3 stoppage will result, owing to too many cartridges having fallen down.

(c) If the rim is broken so that the cartridge is not able to leave the magazine, a No. 3 stoppage will probably result.

7. *Piston rod, broken.—*The gun may fire for a considerable time with this breakage. Eventually it will fire erratically, and finally stop, owing to the burring up of the broken ends.

8. *Rebound pawl, worn or broken.—*Gun will probably fire single shots, stopping in No. 1 position.

9. *Striker or striker post, broken.—*The mechanism may jamb in any position.

10. *Stop pawl and spring.—*If the stop pawl or its spring are worn, a No. 3 position may occur. If it is broken, gun will probably stop in No. 1 position, and cocking handle cannot be drawn back more than 2 or 3 inches.

11. *Bulged rounds and separated cases.—*These occur so rarely that it is only necessary to set them up once for instructional purposes. They usually give a position "in front of trigger," but a badly bulged round may cause a fault in feed (No. 3 position). Bulged rounds are cleared by means of a lanyard placed on the cocking handle. Separated cases cleared by means of a clearing plug. If no clearing plug is available, reload and press trigger—the obstruction will probably adhere to the next cartridge. If it does not, increase tension of return spring and repeat.

12. *Long ammunition.—*If the third position occurs frequently, and it cannot be traced to any of the " probable causes," remove the magazine, and examine the position of the cartridge. If bullet is bearing against front of cartridge slot in the body—

ammunition is too long. If the front of the cartridge slot is sloped off downwards this stoppage will not occur.

13. *To avoid alteration of weight of return spring.*—When stripping to clear a stoppage, the pistol grip should be replaced with the cocking handle in the same position as when commencing to strip.

The best rule to follow is that whenever possible the cocking handle must be *forward* before the pistol grip is withdrawn or replaced.

14. When the gun stops with the cocking handle in the forward position and the magazine rotates freely, the magazine is empty.

Setting up Stoppages.

When practising stoppages firers should be in the prone position, butt in the shoulder. They should try magazine and pull back cocking handle without removing the butt from the shoulder, and recognize the position of the cocking handle without looking at it.

Cause.	In Barracks.	On Range.
Misfire.	Load and press the trigger.	Place dummy round in magazine.
Worn or broken striker.	Load and press trigger but gun still won't fire.	Place two dummy rounds in magazine
Worn or broken feed pawl or feed pawl spring.	Remove feed pawl spring.	Remove feed pawl spring.
Damaged magazine.	Use damaged magazine.	Use damaged magazine.
Hard extraction.	Replace an empty case partly in chamber.	
Friction in gas cylinder.	Withdraw cocking handle far enough to eject an empty case, but not far enough for bolt to engage behind a fresh round.	Remove gas regulator key and turn regulator slightly.
Weak cartridge guide spring	Press down nose of cartridge and allow bolt to go forward. Replace magazine.	
Broken cartridge guide spring.	Remove, or use a broken, cartridge guide spring.	Remove, or use a broken, cartridge guide spring.
Broken extractors.	Load and place an empty case in the chamber.	Load and place an empty case in chamber.
Broken ejector.	Remove ejector.	Remove ejector.

SECTION 9.

Elementary Drill.

During drill, dummies will be used, but great care must be taken that only those with wooden bullets are used.

Carrier containing four magazines placed on left of gun at two paces interval.

Command—" Fall in."

Squad falls in in single rank, five paces in front of gun.

Command—" Number."

As usual.

Command—" Take Post."

Squad turns to right and doubles round behind gun.

No. 1. (*a*) Takes up position on left of gun.
     (*b*) Takes off cover and examines gun.
     (*c*) Takes magazine from No. 2 and places it on gun.
     (*d*) Reports " Ready."

No. 2. (*a*) Takes up position on left of carrier.
     (*b*) Examines the magazines.
     (*c*) Hands one magazine to No. 1, and closes carrier.
        After this No. 1 repeats all words of command.

On the command—" Action, Range, Object " :—

No. 1. (*a*) Adjusts the sights to the range ordered, then lowers leaf.
     (*b*) Runs forward and gets into a firing position on the position indicated.
     (*c*) Raises leaf, rotates magazine, and pulls back cocking handle.

No. 2. Runs forward and when No. 1 is in position, lies down on left of gun and takes one magazine out of carrier.
     When No. 1 is ready to fire, No. 2 holds out his hand and watches Commander.

Signal—" Fire."

No. 2 touches No. 1.

No. 1 presses trigger and fires in bursts of about one second, relaying after each burst, but allowing cocking handle to remain forward.

NOTE.—*If fire is not opened within 3 seconds of the signal, instructors must take steps to ascertain the reason of the delay.*

Command—" Change."

No. 1 grips magazine with right hand, releasing catch with thumb.

No. 2 helps to lift off empty magazine by pressing up centre block with left hand, and puts full magazine on gun with right,

pressing it down. No. 1 passes empty magazine upside down *under* gun to No. 2, pulls full magazine in the feeding direction and pulls back cocking handle. He then relays and continues firing.
Signal—" Cease Fire."

    No. 1 (a) raises safety catch. (In drill, cocking handle must first be pulled back.)

        (b) if magazine is nearly empty, replaces with full one.

    NOTE.—*Before dropping safety catch again, pull back cocking handle.*

Signal—" Out of Action."

    No. 1 (a) unloads, *i.e.*, removes magazine in the usual manner, pulls back cocking handle, takes aim and presses the trigger. Then lowers leaf of back sight.

        (b) retires with gun to cover (at drill, to original position).

    No. 2 (a) helps No. 1 to unload, and replaces magazine in carrier.

        (b) retires to cover with No. 1.

    NOTE.—*To save time in drill the command ' Unload" may sometimes be given instead of signal " out of action." Nos. 1 and 2 then perform actions (a) only.*

SECTION 10.

Tests of Elementary Training.

  (i) " Action," time 10 secs. Points to be observed, sights upright and approximately aligned. Length of run, 5 yards.

 (ii) " Change magazine," time 3 secs. Each motion done distinctly. New magazine rotated.

(iii) Magazine filling by hand, time 1 min. 15 secs.

SECTION 11.

Notes on Range Work.

1. In cases where circumstances make it impossible to carry out the full practices laid down in *Addendum No. 2 to Musketry Regulations*, the following short practices are suggested :—

(i) Grouping	....	....	....	....	6	rounds.
(ii) Repetition	....	....	....	....	6	,,
(iii) Application	....	....	....	....	12	,,
(iv) Swing Traverse	....	....	....	....	20	,,
(v) Practical Rectification of Stoppages			....		30	,,

2. Strict drill discipline will always be maintained on the range.

3. Points before, during and after firing will always be carried out by members of the squads—supervised by instructors.

4. The first firer of each practice will be instructed by the instructor in the presence of the whole squad. That firer afterwards instructs the next firer—supervised by the instructor.

5. Groups must be separate and distinct on the target; they should be within the horizontal bands.

6. No groups—or shots from the swing traverse—should be low enough on the target to go through the figures.

7. Conduct of practices :—

 (i) *Grouping.*—Criticise from gun position—by means of field glasses—after each group. Before the target is patched out each group should be further criticised, in the presence of the firer, at the target, by the Officer or N.C.O. who conducted the practice.

 (ii) *Repetition.*—All who fail to make a reasonable group at the first attempt will repeat (if time permits) after the whole squad has completed that practice. The practice will be conducted as for practice (i), supervised by the Staff Sergeant.

 (iii) *Application.*—The fire orders for both groups will be given before fire is opened. Particular attention should be paid to the time elapsing between the groups and the position of the second group chiefly criticised. If observation of the group is difficult, an observer with field glasses may be allowed. Criticism at gun position and target will be carried out as for practice (i).

 (iv) *Swing Traverse.*—Before commencing to fire, each firer will be given two timed practice swings. Time allowed to swing across target—from left figure to right figure, 6 seconds. The ammunition allotted will sweep about two-thirds of the target, but the swing should be continued to the right figure. Criticism as above.

 (v) *Stoppages.*—Note 5 will be adhered to also in stoppages. The No. 2 on the gun will always be in possession of the necessary spare parts, &c.

APPENDIX I.

List of Equipment, with Spare Parts, Tools and Appurtenances for the Lewis Gun. (War Office letter 79/7881 (A.3.) of 8.5.16).

WOOLWICH SECTION 16—B.

Components.

Gun, Lewis, ·303-*inch :—*	
Barrel ..	1
Blades, foresight, high	1
,, ,, low	1
Bolt (assembled, with two extractors and one feed arm actuating stud)	1
Casting, pinion (assembled complete)	1
Cylinder, gas ..	1
Ejector	1
Extractors ..	4
Handle, cocking	2
Head, screw, tangent sight ..	1
Key, gas, regulator ..	1
Magazines ..	64*
Pawl, feed arm	1
,, ·pinion ..	1
,, stop, magazine, left ..	1
,, ,, ,, right	1
Pin, axis, pawl, pinion	1
,, ,, sear	1
,, ,, trigger ..	1
,, fixing head, screw, tangent sight	2
,, striker ..	2
,, locking body ..	1
Regulator, gas	1
Rod, piston, complete	1
Screw, clamp ring ..	1
Sear	1
Spring, guide, cartridge	12†
,, head, screw, tangent sight..	2
,, pawl, feed arm	3
,, ,, pinion..	2
,, pawls, stop, magazine	3
,, return (with retaining collar)	2
,, trigger	1
Striker..	2

Tools and Appurtenances.

Gun, Lewis, ·303-*inch :—*	
Brush, wire, rod, cleaning, cylinder	2
Handle, loading, magazines..	10
,, wood ..	1

---

* Number of magazines per gun now reduced to 44.

† In the case of the stronger new pattern cartridge guide springs (now in general use), the number is reduced to 6.

Gun, Lewis, ·303-inch—contd.

Mop, rod, cleaning cylinder..	2
Plug, clearing..	1
Rod, cleaning, cylinder	1
Spanner, mouthpiece, barrel	2

Guns, Maxim and Lewis, ·303-inch :—

Balance, spring, M.G.	1
Box, tin, small parts, M.G...	1
Hammer, M.G.	1
Pliers, cutting, M.G.	1
Punch, No. 4, M.G. ..	1
Reflector, mirror, M.G.	1
Rod, cleaning, M.G...	1
Screwdriver, large, M.G.	1
,, small, M.G.	1
Wallet, case, spare parts box (Mark I)	1

Guns, Vickers and Lewis, ·303-inch :—

Can, oil	1

WEEDON SECTIONS.

Gauze, wire, pieces	2
Pull-through, double	1

COMPLETE LIST OF COMPONENT PARTS OF THE LEWIS ·303-INCH GUN.

Arm, feed (with latch).
Band, barrel
Barrel.
Bed, tangent sight.
Body.
Bolt.
Butt.
Cap, butt.
Casing pinion
,, radiator, front.
,, ,, rear.
,, return spring.
Catch, butt.
Mouthpiece, barrel.
Pawl, feed arm.
,, pinion.
,, stop, magazine, right.
,, ,, ,, left.
Pin, axis, leaf, tangent sight.
,, ,, pawl, pinion.
,, ,, sear.
,, ,, trigger.
,, fixing, rack, piston rod.
,, striker.
,, hinge, pinion casing.
,, keeper, butt catch.
Chamber, gas.
Cover body
,, ejector.

Pin, fixing, head, screw.
,, tangent sight.
,, locking body.
,, split, keeper, axis pin, tangent sight.
Pinion.
Plate, butt.
,, safety catch, right
,, ,, ,, left.
Plunger, spring, trigger.
Radiator.
Regulator, gas.
Ring, clamp.
Rod, piston.
Screw, bed and spring, tangent sight.
,, butt plate (2).
Screw, butt cap.
,, clamp ring.
,, elevating, tangent sight
,, tension, return spring.
Sear.
Side-piece, pistol grip, right.
,, ,, ,, left.
Slide, tangent sight.
Spring, butt catch.
,, cartridge guide.
,, head, screw, tangent sight.
,, pawl, feed arm.

Cylinder, gas
Ejector.
Extractors (2).
Foresight.
Guard, trigger (and pistol grip)
Handle, cocking.
Head, screw, elevating tangent sight.
Hub, return spring.
Key, gas regulator.
Latch, feed arm.
Leaf, tangent sight.
Magazine

Spring, pawl pinion.
   ,,   pawls, stop, magazine.
   ,,   return.
   ,,   tangent sight.
   ,,   trigger.
Striker.
Stud, axis, latch, feed arm.
   ,,   actuating, feed arm.
   ,,   positioning, clamp ring.
Trigger.
Washer, pin, axis, tangent sight.

ADDITIONAL EQUIPMENT FOR LEWIS GUNS, AUTHORIZED BY G.R.Os. FOR ISSUE IN FRANCE.

	G.R.O.	Date.
Rimers for use with Lewis guns : issue of one per unit	1210	13.10.15
Pistols, Very, 1-inch	1263	17,11.15
Handles loading magazine : additional issue to complete scale of 10 per gun	1328	20.12.15
Paint for casings, Lewis guns : issue on scale of 1 pint per battalion	1339	27.12.15
Hyposcopes for Lewis guns : issue on scale of one per two guns	1442	3.3.16
Cover for protection of working parts	1608	30.5.16
Canvas carriers for holding magazines : 11 per gun	1695	18.7.16
Stick carborundum, triangular ¾-inch, fine, for removal of sharp edges or burrs in working parts	1747	18.8.16
Slings, Lewis guns : issue of one per gun for carrying when hot	1967	25.11.16
Cartridges, dummy, wooden ; cartridges, dummy, steel, two per gun (for instructional purposes)	2065	7.1.17

EQUIPMENT AUTHORIZED BY G.H.Q. LETTERS.

	Letter.	Date.
Revolvers for Nos. 1 and 2 of Lewis gun detachments	O.B./407	7.7.16
*Number of handcarts reduced to one per gun ..	O.B./896	15.10.16

*As soon as limbered wagons are available for Lewis guns (one wagon per 4 guns), the handcarts will be withdrawn.

Articles Useful to Lewis Gunners Issued to Battalions.

—	Authority.	Date.
Binoculars, issued on scale of 2 prismatic and 38 ordinary per battalion	A.F.G. 1098/110 ..	—
Range finders, Barr and Stroud or Marindin : issued on scale of 5 per battalion	A.F.G. 1098/110 ..	—
Phosphorescent night-sights : issue on scale of 64 per battalion, together with 1 yard of magnesium wire (spare), per sight	G.R.O. 831 ..	6.5.
Lamps, brazing, 1 pint : scale of issue one per battalion, for use of armourer sergeant in carrying out repairs	G.R.O. 1081 ..	13.6.15

Lewis Gun Equipment Noted in "Lists of Changes in War Matériel."

(Approved but not Authorized for General Issue on Regular Scale.)

—	Number.	Date.
Gun, Lewis : washer, packing barrel, steel ·005-inch, for taking up play between rear radiator casing and body in old guns	17674	1.4.16
Gun, Lewis : butt, short (approved for Bantam battalions)	17713	1.5.16
Box, magazines for two carriers and one handle, loading ..	17739	1.6.16
*Spring, guide cartridge, new pattern with spring ..	17769	1.7.16

* This stronger pattern is now practically universal.

APPENDIX II.

Instructions to Armourers for the Modification of Pinion Casings to facilitate removal.

The following alteration, which can be carried out by any armourer, enables the old pattern pinion casing to be removed without touching the body-locking pin, and so greatly reduces the time needed for changing a broken return spring :—

$$\text{Authority } \frac{\text{O.S.M./274}}{\text{Q./1538/4/S.P.}} \text{ of } 16/8/16.$$

On the projection of casing forming the hinge, a small semi-circular groove will be made by filing away the metal at the position shown in sketch. Only sufficient to clear the body-locking pin should be removed.

To test if correctly modified :—When changing the casing it should only be necessary (1) to remove butt-stock ; (2) to draw back the trigger guard slightly.

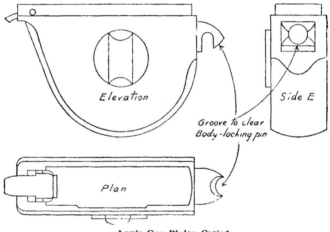

Elevation

Side E

Groove to clear
Body-locking pin

Plan

Lewis Gun Pinion Casing.

APPENDIX III.

Transport of Lewis Guns and Ammunition.

As soon as four limbered G.S. wagons for transport of Lewis guns are available for each infantry battalion, one will be allotted to each company for its four guns.   This company wagon will be loaded as follows :—

	Lbs.
4 Lewis guns, at 27 lbs.	108
4 gun chests, at 33 lbs.	132
4 sets spare parts, complete, at 15 lbs. ..	60
176 magazines, filled, at 4½ lbs.	792
22 tin magazine boxes, at 8¼ lbs. (each holding 8 magazines in 2 carriers)..	182
9,000 rounds, S.A.A. (in boxes of 1,000 rounds, at 75 lbs.)	675
Total	1,949

This load represents, per gun, 2,068 rounds in magazines and 2,250 rounds packed in chargers.

In addition, 2,000 rounds per gun are carried by the Divisional Ammunition Column.